Symbols of Freedom

National Parks

Carlsbad Caverns National Park

M.C. Hall

Heinemann Library
Chicago, Illinois

Customer Service 888-454-2279
Visit our website at www.heinemannlibrary.com

Page layout by Ron Kamen and edesign
Photo research by Maria Joannou and Erica Newbery
Illustrations by Martin Sanders
Printed and bound in China by South China Printing Company Limited

10 09 08 07 06
10 9 8 7 6 5 4 3 2 1

Library of Congress Cataloging-in-Publication Data
Hall, Margaret, 1947-
  Carlsbad Caverns National Park / M.C. Hall.
      p. cm. -- (Symbols of freedom)
Includes bibliographical references and index.
ISBN 1-4034-7792-2 (library binding - hardcover)
1. Carlsbad Caverns (N.M.)--Juvenile literature. 2. Carlsbad Caverns National Park (N.M.)--Juvenile literature. I. Title. II. Series.
   F802.C28H35 2006
   978.9'42--dc22

                      2005025734

Acknowledgments
The author and publishers are grateful to the following for permission to reproduce copyright material:
Alamy Images pp. **7** (David South), **10** (Andre Jenny), **24** (Andy Jackson), **27** (Bruce Coleman Inc.); Corbis pp. **4** (Buddy Mays), **5** (William A. Bake), **9**, **11** (Danny Lehman), **14** (David Muench), **23** (Buddy Mays), **25** (Lynda Richardson), **26** (Lowell Georgia); Geoscience p. **22**; Getty Images p. **12** (National Geographic/Richard Nowitz); Library of Congress p. **19**; Lonely Planet Images p. **13** (John Elk III); National Parks Service p. **21**; National Parks Service/Photograph by Peter Jones pp. **15**, **16**, **17**, **18**, **20**; Northwind Picture Archive p. **8**.

Cover photograph of Carlsbad Caverns National Park reproduced with permission of Corbis/Richard T. Nowitz. The Publishers would like to thank the staff of Carlsbad Caverns National Park for their assistance in the preparation of this book.

Every effort has been made to contact copyright holders of any material reproduced in this book. Any omissions will be rectified in subsequent printings if notice is given to the publisher.

Some words are shown in bold, **like this**. You can find out what they mean by looking in the glossary.

Contents

Our National Parks 4

Carlsbad Caverns National Park 6

Carlsbad Caverns Long Ago 8

Visiting Carlsbad Caverns
    National Park 10

The Caverns 12

Cave Formations 14

Entering the Caverns 16

Inside the Big Room 18

Other Caves 20

Desert Plants and Animals 22

Cave Plants and Animals 24

Millions of Bats 26

Map of Carlsbad Caverns
    National Park 28

Timeline 29

Glossary 30

Find Out More 31

Index 32

National parks are areas of land set aside for people to visit and enjoy. These parks do not belong to one person. They belong to everyone in the United States.

People like to hike in national parks.

There are **388** national park areas in the United States. Carlsbad Caverns National Park is very unusual. The park's most interesting sights are deep inside the earth.

Carlsbad Caverns National Park

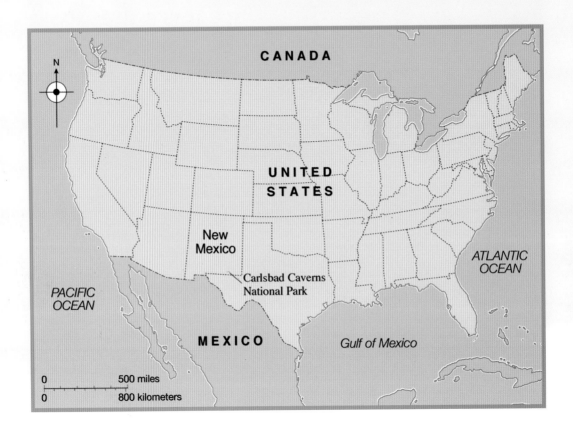

Carlsbad Caverns National Park is in the southeastern corner of the state of New Mexico. The park includes more than 100 underground **caverns**.

The land above the caverns is part of the Chihuahuan Desert. There are few roads in this area. Most of the park is a **wilderness**, with rocky hills and **canyons**.

Carlsbad Caverns Long Ago

Long ago, Native Americans lived near Carlsbad Caverns. In the 1800s, cowboys came to the area to raise cattle. A cowboy named Jim White explored the **caverns.**

The Mescalero Apaches lived near the caverns.

In 1915, Jim White took photographers into the caverns. Their pictures made people want to visit and protect the area. In 1930, Carlsbad Caverns became a **national park**.

Visiting Carlsbad Caverns National Park

In the winter, it gets cold enough to snow in the Chihuahuan Desert. Spring is very windy and stormy. Most visitors come in the summer, when the weather is hot and dry.

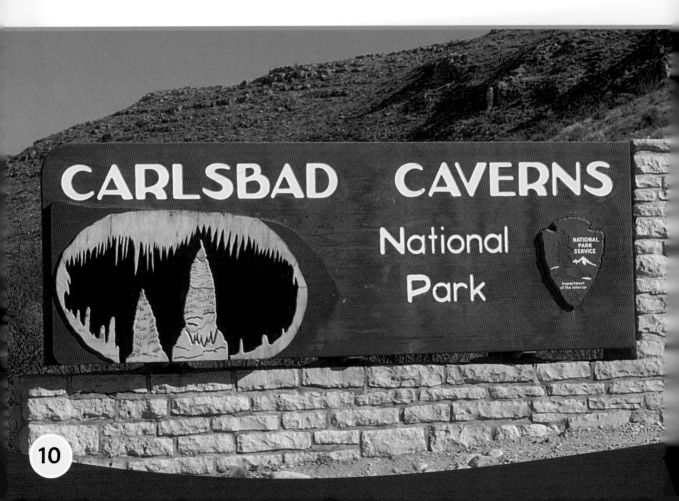

Inside the **caverns**, the weather does not matter. The temperature under the ground does not change. Visitors can explore the caverns at any time of the year.

Even on a hot day, it is cool inside the caverns.

The Caverns

The **caverns** are formed from a type of rock called **limestone**. Water got into cracks in the rocks and **dissolved** some of the limestone.

After millions of years, the water created hollow spaces called caverns.

Some caverns are tiny. Others are huge. In places, water has flowed into the caves and formed pools.

Trickling water has created amazing rock shapes.

Cave Formations

Water is always dripping into the **caverns**. Each drip leaves **minerals** behind. After millions of years, minerals pile up to make strange shapes called **formations**.

This formation has been named The Temple of the Sun.

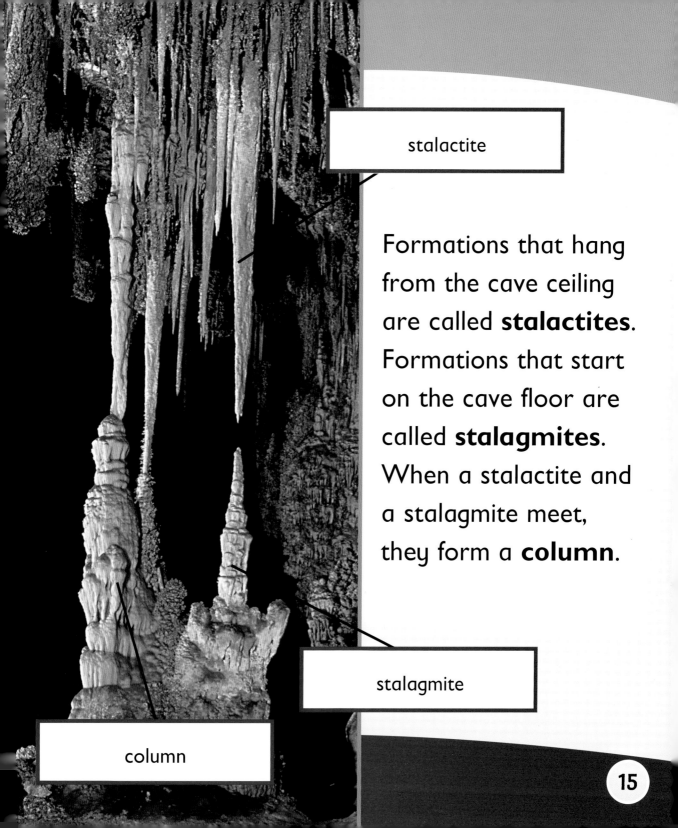

stalactite

Formations that hang from the cave ceiling are called **stalactites**. Formations that start on the cave floor are called **stalagmites**. When a stalactite and a stalagmite meet, they form a **column**.

stalagmite

column

15

Entering the Caverns

A large hole called the Natural Entrance leads to a steep, winding trail. The trail ends about a mile later at a rest area far below the ground.

There are many interesting **formations** on the trail.

Visitors can also reach the rest area by elevator. From there it is an easy walk to the Big Room.

The Big Room is so huge that more than six football fields could fit on its floor!

 # Inside the Big Room

A trail goes around the edges of the Big Room. There are many interesting **formations** to see. One looks like a lion's tail hanging from the ceiling.

These formations almost reach the top of the cavern.

Park rangers walk around the Big Room. They answer visitors' questions about the **caverns**. They also make sure that visitors stay safe.

Some of the caves of Carlsbad Caverns are not easy to see. **Park rangers** lead people into these caves. In places, the only way to get up or down is by climbing a ladder or using a rope.

There are also **wild caves** at Carlsbad Caverns. A wild cave is one with no trails or electric lights. Visitors can only go into these caves with a park ranger.

You must carry lights in a wild cave.

Above ground, most of Carlsbad Caverns National Park is desert. Cactus, thorny bushes, and twisted piñon pine trees also grow in the park.

Plants like this can survive in the desert, where there is little rain.

Wild boar also live in the park.

Many mule deer live in the park. So do coyotes, mountain lions, and small mammals like rabbits and squirrels. The desert is also home to rattlesnakes and the spadefoot toad.

Cave Plants and Animals

Visitors often do not notice anything living in the **caverns**. However, tiny **bacteria** live in underground pools of water. Plants called **fungi** live on rocks in the dark caves.

Fungi do not need sunlight to grow or make food.

Animals also live in the caves. Cave crickets use their **antennae** to move around in the dark. Cave swallows make their nests in caverns.

Millions of Bats

Mexican free-tailed bats live in the park from spring until winter. In the early evening, visitors gather outside the Bat Cave to see the bats.

The park is famous for this bat flight.

The bats sleep all day. When it starts to get dark, they leave to catch insects. Millions of bats fly out of the cave at once. In the morning, they fly back inside.

Map of Carlsbad Caverns National Park

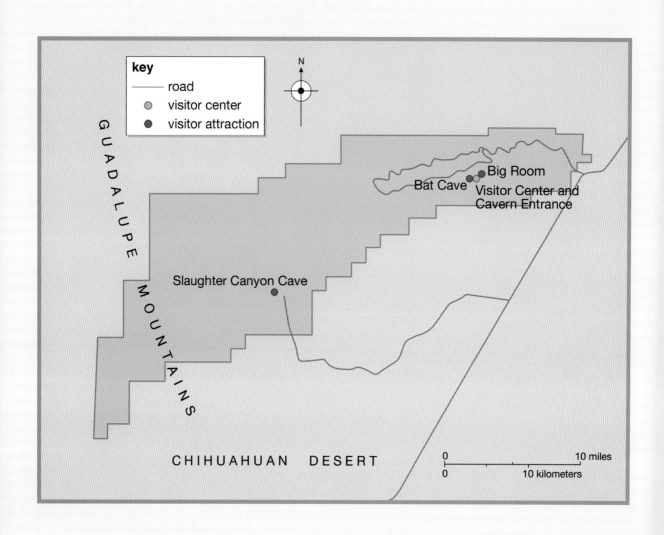

key
— road
● visitor center
● visitor attraction

N

GUADALUPE MOUNTAINS

Bat Cave

Big Room

Visitor Center and Cavern Entrance

Slaughter Canyon Cave

CHIHUAHUAN DESERT

0   10 miles
0   10 kilometers

Timeline

Thousands of years ago	Native Americans live on land above Carlsbad Caverns.
1898	Jim White probably enters the caves for the first time and scratches his name into the rock.
1915	Jim White takes photographers into the caves.
1923	Carlsbad Caves National Monument is established to protect the caves.
1923–1927	Trails, stairs, and lights are added to the caves.
1930	Carlsbad Caverns becomes a **national park**.
1939	Slaughter Canyon and parts of the Chihuahuan Desert are added to the park.
1978	Carlsbad Caverns National Park is named as a **wilderness** area.
1986	Cavers explore Leghuguilla Cave, one of the largest caves in the world.
1995	Carlsbad Caverns National Park becomes a World Heritage Site.

# Glossary

antennae body part on an insect's head used for feeling, smelling, and touching

bacteria tiny living things that can only be seen through microscopes. They are not plants or animals.

canyon steep-sided valley

cavern hollowed-out space

column tall, thick formation

dissolve to break down in water

formation something made or created

fungi plants that do not need sunlight to grow

limestone rock made from shells pressing together for millions of years

minerals solid materials that are not plants or animals. Most rocks are made of combinations of minerals.

national park natural area set aside for people to visit

park ranger person who works in a national park and shares information about the wildlife and unusual sites of the park

stalactite formation that hangs down from the ceiling of a cave

stalagmite formation that rises from the cave floor

wild cave cave that does not have trails or lights to help people explore it

wilderness area that is wild and natural

Find Out More

Books
An older reader can help you with these books:

Aulenbach, Nancy H. *Exploring Caves: Journeys into the Earth.*
    Washington, D.C.: National Geographic, 2001.
Burnham, Brad. *Carlsbad Caverns: America's Largest Underground
    Chamber. Famous Caves of the World Series.* New York, NY:
    Rosen Publishing Group, 2003.
Harrison, David. *Caves: Mysteries Below Our Feet. Earthworks
    Series.* Boyds Mills, PA: Boyds Mills Press, 2001.

Address
To find out more about Carlsbad Caverns National Park,
write to:

Carlsbad Caverns National Park
3225 National Parks Highway
Carlsbad, NM 88220
Tel: (505) 785-2232

Website
http://www.nps.gov/cave

From this site you can take tours around some of the
famous caverns.

Index

animals 23, 25, 26–27

bacteria 24
bats 25, 26–27
Big Room 17, 18, 19

canyons 7
caverns 6, 8, 9, 11–21, 24–25, 29
Chihuahuan Desert 7, 10, 29
columns 15

formations 14–15, 16, 18
fungi 24

limestone 12

national parks 4–5, 9
Native Americans 8, 29

New Mexico 6

park rangers 19, 20, 21
plants 22, 24
pools 13

stalactites 15
stalagmites 15
summer 10

visitor center 10

White, Jim 8, 9, 29
wild caves 21
wilderness 7, 29
winter 10